IMAGES
of America

BETHEL

OLD HOME DAY, JULY 4, 1910. This gathering of schoolchildren atop Hoyt's Hill once appeared as a supplement to the *New York Sunday World.*

IMAGES
of America

BETHEL

Patrick Tierney Wild

ARCADIA

First published 1996
Copyright © Patrick Tierney Wild, 1996

ISBN 0-7524-0476-8

Published by Arcadia Publishing,
an imprint of the Chalford Publishing Corporation
One Washington Center, Dover, New Hampshire 03820
Printed in Great Britain

Library of Congress Cataloging-in-Publication Data applied for

*This book is respectfully dedicated to all individuals living and dead
who ever called Bethel, Connecticut, "home."*

Contents

Acknowledgments

This book would not have been possible without the cooperation and contribution of many different individuals and organizations. The bulk of photographs reproduced in this publication were graciously loaned by the Bethel Historical Society. Special thanks go to Timothy Beeble, the society's president, and Lillian Emmons, the society's vice-president. The Scott-Fanton Museum of Danbury also provided essential photographs and thanks should be bestowed to Maryann Root and Kathleen Zuris for their wonderful help in locating them. They and their institution provide a vital service to all who enjoy history. Clifford Hurgin, our town's former first selectman, was of enormous assistance in providing both photographs and historical background for many of the images. Appreciation is expressed to Mr. and Mrs. Lewis Goodsell Jr. for their contribution of photographs that had been collected over the years by Lewis Goodsell Sr. and his wife Laura. Mrs. Judith Hatch has generously contributed both photographs and background material hitherto unseen in any work concerning Bethel. Her efforts were of tremendous importance. Thanks is extended to the Connecticut State Library and its employees for their assistance in reproducing Bethel scenes culled from the Clark Photograph Collection. Mr. Donald Dempsey and his employees at White Light Studios of Bethel are to be thanked for providing the expertise that made it possible to duplicate rare, original photographs. Appreciation is given to Ms. Alice Knapp, town librarian, who shared some of her recent historical finds. Mr. George M. Hoyt provided photographs belonging to his family and Mr. Ed English and Paul English obligingly did as well. Lastly, my greatest thanks is awarded to my wife, Alexa, who has put up with my "obsessing" over Bethel history for many years now. She has always been my greatest supporter and most trusted assistant. Without her this book might never have seen the light of day.

Introduction

Ever since Bethel broke away from the larger neighboring town of Danbury, Connecticut, it has suffered from somewhat of an inferiority complex concerning its history. Because Bethel was part of Danbury from its founding in 1684 up until Bethel's incorporation by the state assembly in 1855, most Bethelites simply accepted the idea that Bethel's history was essentially Danbury's history. Consequently, since Danbury's history has been extensively documented, there was no need to add anything further. However, this viewpoint did not take into account that Bethel has always had its own unique identity both before and after its separation from its mother town. For example, Danbury, Connecticut, was long touted as the "Hat Capital of the World." Few people realize that at certain points in history, Bethel hat factories outnumbered those in the "Hat City," and at one point in the 1960s Danbury had no operating hat factories while Bethel did. This is only one small example of the importance of documenting the history of our town through the use of historic photographs.

The story is told of how members of eight Norwalk, Connecticut, families walked to the area now known as Danbury and Bethel in the summer of 1684. Legend has it that one of their number, namely John Hoyt, was sent ahead as a scout to find suitable ground for a settlement. Hoyt reputedly passed his first night in our area, sleeping beneath a rock at the base of what has come to be known as Hoyt's Hill. Although these first European settlers chose the area now constituting Danbury's Main Street as the spot to establish themselves, they had laid their eyes on Bethel. The first colonists to reside on land now within Bethel's boundaries most likely arrived sometime around 1700 and may have set up housekeeping in the part of town now known as Grassy Plain. This seems likely given the area's close proximity to the initial settlement site at the corner of South and Main Streets in Danbury.

By 1759 there were enough families in Danbury that overcrowding was a problem at the only house of worship, that of the Congregationalists. So it was that in April of that same year several parishioners living in the eastern portion of Danbury petitioned the General Assembly of the Colony of Connecticut to have their portion of Danbury set off as a second parish. Although not all of the parishioners were in agreement on this endeavor, the general assembly granted the request the following October and the First Ecclesiastical Society of Bethel was formally organized on November 12, 1759. Over the next ninety-six years, the parish of Bethel tried several times to establish itself as a town in its own right, but none of these attempts proved successful. Finally, on June 21, 1855, after a successful campaign led by state representative and resident Oliver Shepard, Bethel officially became Connecticut's 154th town.

Well before 1855, the town had seen one industry come to dominate its economy: hatting.

The earliest documented evidence of hatting can be found in a ledger book now on file in the archives of the Connecticut State Library. There we find the ledger book of Thomas Taylor containing an initial entry that reads: "December 4th, 1789—I began the hat(t)ing business—glover Mansfield for my workman." Although other industries, such as comb-making (utilizing cowhorn) and shoe-making, were at one point important activities, the manufacture of hats for men, women, and children provided the axis on which all activity in Bethel would revolve until the last facility run by the Barton Rough Hat Company closed in the mid-1960s.

Another highlight of our town's history is that the great showman, P.T. Barnum, was born here on July 5, 1810. Barnum remained in town only until the age of twenty-four, but during his stay he managed to run a successful country store, operate a lottery, publish the town's first newspaper, and also spend sixty days in the Danbury jail on a libel conviction. In later life Barnum made frequent visits to his hometown in order to visit his family and friends. On one such visit in August of 1881, Barnum presented his birthplace with an enormous bronze fountain that would serve as the town's centerpiece for the next forty-two years.

In the mid-nineteenth to early twentieth centuries, Bethel adopted technological advances and expanded its civic facilities. The railroad first came to town in 1852, connecting Bethel to Norwalk and the growing metropolis of New York City. Another line known as the Shepaug Railroad connecting link was established in 1872, enabling Bethelites to travel to the northern town of Litchfield (this line was discontinued in 1911). A town-supplied water system was created in 1879 utilizing the Eureka Reservoir, and electricity began to be available in the late 1880s (although many townspeople would not have their homes electrified until the 1920s). A horse-drawn trolley system was inaugurated in 1887 and continued service until January 1, 1895, when it was replaced by an extended electric trolley line that would continue to operate until 1926. A permanent home for a public library was found in 1914 through the generous donation made by the Seelye family of their old homestead on Greenwood Avenue. A public high school was first built on South Street in 1887 to service the increasing number of scholars who pursued their studies beyond the eighth grade.

In conclusion, it must be stated that this photographic chronicle of Bethel's history from 1860 to the 1950s does not claim to be the ultimate record of our town's past, but it is the best and most extensive collection of historic photographs yet to be assembled. It is hoped that its pages will prove informative and entertaining for years to come.

One
All Around the Town

GREENWOOD AVENUE, 1907. Traffic was not a problem when this photograph was taken. The area shown to the right is now occupied by the entrance to Dolan Plaza. The town's primary thoroughfare was still a dirt road at this time; however, cobblestones were placed between the trolley tracks.

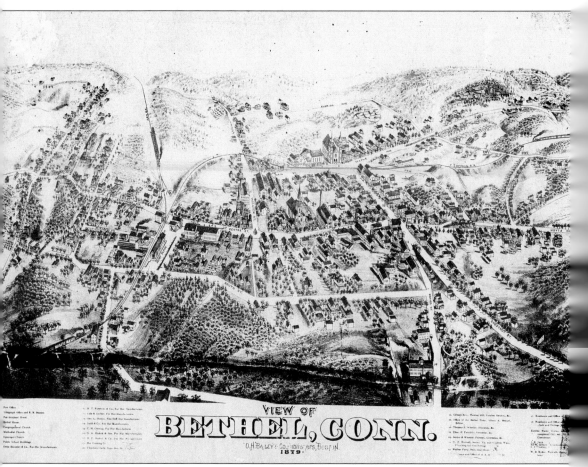

A BIRD'S-EYE VIEW OF BETHEL, 1879. This amusing interpretation of Bethel was created by O.H. Bailey & Company of Boston. The attention to detail is remarkable, although in some cases items considered unattractive—such as outhouses or trees that would have obscured buildings—have been deleted. Notice also that there are three trains headed for each other on the same track.

MAIN STREET, *c.* 1910. This scene shows the area just in front of the Second Meeting House, now home to the Bethel Historical Society and the Veterans of Foreign Wars. The tracks of the Shepaug Railroad connecting link can be seen running along the north side of the street.

MAIN STREET, *c.* 1910. An army unit once staged training exercises in the Elmwood section of town and was encamped across from King Lake. A single-engine biplane that was part of their equipment crashed in the Taunton Hill section of Newtown. Soldiers can be seen unloading their wagons from railroad cars stopped in front of the Congregational church.

GREENWOOD AVENUE, 1909. The town's "toonerville trolley"—which ran from the railroad crossing to the intersection of Greenwood Avenue and Milwaukee Avenue—can be seen at right. The Barnum fountain can be seen at center on the spot now occupied by the doughboy statue. At the time, this section of Greenwood Avenue was called Centre (or Center) Street and P.T. Barnum Square was known as Fountain Place.

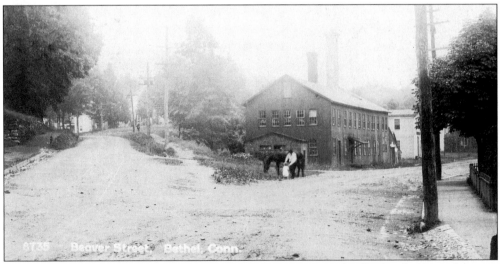

NASHVILLE ROAD AND CHESTNUT STREET, 1911. Nashville Road was at this time known as Beaver Street. The large building shown to the right is the Heyman Hat Factory. Behind the hat factory can be seen the tall hose tower that was once attached to the Alert Hose Company's firehouse, now occupied by the Grassy Plain Drum Corps.

GREENWOOD AVENUE, 1911. This photograph was apparently taken immediately after a rainstorm, as the sidewalks are wet and the street is somewhat muddy. A sign for English's Drug Store can be seen at left and the front entrance to the Methodist church can be seen at right.

GREENWOOD AVENUE, c. 1925. The automobile was by now making its appearance in larger numbers. The majority of the commercial buildings shown on the south side of the street still stand today.

13

GREENWOOD AVENUE, 1913. When this postcard was produced an electric sign welcoming visitors to town was stretched across the roadway between what is now the Bethel Public Library and the opera house. The large Victorian-style home to the left was torn down in 1959 to make way for what is now the First Union Bank.

Greenwood Avenue, Bethel, Conn.

GREENWOOD AVENUE, c. 1915. A magnificent canopy of elm trees lined the street at the time this postcard was produced. The small white sign at left probably warned travelers that they were approaching the spot where the trolley made its turnabout. To the right can be seen a large horse-pulled lawn-mowing apparatus of the period.

GREENWOOD AVENUE RAILROAD CROSSING, c. 1930. The Gem Lunch Counter, shown at left, was a popular local eatery at this time. The building on the right was then occupied by Morrison and Dunham Feed and Grain.

GREENWOOD AVENUE, c. 1915. This postcard shows the area at which Beach Street connects with Greenwood Avenue. Other than the roadway being paved, this spot has changed little over the years.

GREENWOOD AVENUE, 1913. Prior to a 1934 consolidation, the street today known as Greenwood Avenue had four distinct parts. Beginning from east to west, those parts were East Street, Elm Street, Center Street, and Greenwood Avenue. This postcard shows the area where Prospect Street connected with what was then Elm Street.

Elm Street, Bethel, Conn.

GREENWOOD AVENUE, c. 1920. This photograph shows the same scene as the previous one but at a later date. The trolley can be seen in the distance.

GRAND STREET, *c.* 1910. This postcard view shows Grand Street—one of Bethel's most fashionable addresses for more than a century—looking north from Greenwood Avenue.

FOUNTAIN PLACE, *c.* 1900. The gentlemen in the foreground are standing outside the Higson Hat Factory in an area that is today the west side of P.T. Barnum Square. In the background can be seen a bandstand that once stood on a grass island located at the intersection of Main and Wooster Streets.

GREENWOOD AVENUE, c. 1899. The electric trolley is shown struggling to make its way through town. The building farthest to the right is now located behind the storefront that houses Pickwick Antiques and the H&R Block tax office. This and the following photographs may have been taken immediately following a blizzard in January 1899.

GREENWOOD AVENUE, c. 1899. This scene shows a trolley car that was specially designed to remove snow from the tracks as it makes its way east along Greenwood Avenue. Saint Mary's Roman Catholic Church can be seen in the distance.

GREENWOOD AVENUE, *c.* 1899. The trolley is making its way past the Methodist church and parsonage. The pedestrians shown at right seem to have their work cut out for them in navigating the unshoveled sidewalks.

GREENWOOD AVENUE, *c.* 1899. Two horse-drawn sleds pass on either side of the trolley near the Methodist parsonage. The building at left, topped by a cupola, was radically altered in 1920 and now houses, among other businesses, Dr. Mike's Ice Cream Store.

FOUNTAIN PLACE, 1899. This scene depicts the corner of Rector Street and Greenwood Avenue. The frozen Barnum fountain can be seen to the right. The store identified as the Fountain Place Market is now the site of the San Miguel restaurant.

THE BARNUM FOUNTAIN, c. 1899. Bethelites apparently considered the appearance of the frozen fountain pleasing to the eye. Unfortunately, allowing the fountain to freeze over also led to its demise. The expansion of the ice within the internal portions of the bronze fountain created cracks that ultimately rendered Barnum's gift unusable.

DOWNTOWN BETHEL, c. 1905. A postcard provides a bird's-eye view of downtown Bethel from the area commonly referred to as Overlook Park, just above the lower portion of South Street. The old Center School can be seen at right as well as the two towers of the Congregational church in the background.

DOWNTOWN BETHEL, c. 1906. This postcard view is similar to the one at the top of the page, except that this image was created during a season of full foliage.

DOWNTOWN BETHEL, *c.* 1935. This scene once again depicts a view of Bethel from a vantage point above the lower portion of South Street. Ferry and Manion's Cider Mill can be seen at right near the intersection of Nashville Road and Chestnut Street.

DOWNTOWN BETHEL, 1907. This scene was apparently photographed from Farnam Hill Road looking east toward Hoyt's Hill. The homes in the immediate foreground face High Street.

THE BETHEL GARAGE, c. 1930. The building that now houses the Famous Cleaners and Tailors establishment serviced automobiles at the time this photograph was taken. REO and Desoto motorcars are advertised, as well as Willard storage batteries. The service station shown on the right is now home to the Shannon Brothers Sunoco.

GREENWOOD AVENUE, c. 1928. Although the event recorded in this unmarked photograph cannot be positively identified, it is possible that the picture was taken at the time of the doughboy statue dedication ceremonies in May of 1928. The two buildings shown to the left have been replaced by the P.T. Barnum Square Plaza.

GREENWOOD AVENUE, *c.* 1910. A farmer, with his wagon piled high with hay, allows his horses to drink from an iron cistern located directly in front of Nichol's Opera House. A sign on the front of the opera house advertises the roller-skating rink that was located on its second floor.

Center Street, Bethel, Conn.

GREENWOOD AVENUE, *c.* 1910. This postcard view of downtown Bethel shows a street that appears deserted, with the exception of a lone teamster sitting in his umbrella-covered wagon.

GREENWOOD AVENUE RAILROAD CROSSING, *c.* 1930. This scene includes Mullaney's Newsstand, a landmark that remained in town for decades. Over the years the store was greatly expanded, but the business began in these small, wood-frame buildings close to the railroad tracks. Notice that Library Place had not yet been cut through.

GREENWOOD AVENUE, *c.* 1930. Downtown Bethel had only recently been paved when this photograph was taken. The entrance to Prospect Street can be seen at right. A large building that stood at the southwest corner of Chestnut Street can be seen in the distance. The building was later purchased by the state and demolished to improve traffic flow.

EAST STREET (NOW GREENWOOD AVENUE), c. 1930. This scene depicts the very bottom of Hoyt's Hill Road on its western side. By this point in time, the electric trolley had been replaced by public buses.

BLACKMAN AVENUE, c. 1930. With the exception of the automobiles and the elm trees, Blackman Avenue has changed little in its appearance from the time of this photograph. Saint Mary's rectory can be seen at the opposite end of the street.

SOUTH STREET, c. 1930. This photograph was taken near the corner of Henry Street looking toward the railroad crossing. The absence of traffic would be remarkable by today's standards.

INTERSECTION OF GREENWOOD AVENUE AND GRASSY PLAIN STREET, c. 1930. Grassy Plain Street was almost entirely residential at this time, except for a service station that Bethelites would later come to know as O'Donnell's Garage. A signpost on the traffic island at left read "Welcome to Bethel" on one side, and "Goodbye, Come Again" on the other.

GRASSY PLAIN STREET, *c*. 1930. This photograph was taken near the entrance to Whitney Road looking south on what is now Route 53. Most of the homes on the west side of the street have been converted for commercial use. The third building from the right is now home to Tonelli's Restaurant.

FLEETWOOD AVENUE, *c*. 1930. Automobiles were at a minimum when this photograph was shot. The corner at left is now occupied by the Mobil service station and the corner at right is now home to Fleet Bank.

GRASSY PLAIN STREET, c. 1930. Crossing the street was not a problem in 1930. The saltbox-style house known as the old Starr homestead, which still stands, is on the left. The area to the right of the home is now occupied by Dunkin' Donuts and other businesses.

CHESTNUT STREET AND GREENWOOD AVENUE, 1930. Officer Morris Britto directs traffic at an important intersection in Bethel. The large Victorian-style home at left is currently the site of a Citgo service station.

GREENWOOD AVENUE, *c.* 1910. Bethel's main thoroughfare is shown at the point where it connects with Blackman Avenue. The raised gates of the railroad crossing can be seen in the distance.

EAST STREET (NOW GREENWOOD AVENUE), *c.* 1910. The road leading to the center of Bethel was still dirt when this photograph was taken. Hoyt's Hill Road begins at the lower right-hand corner and Andrews Street can be seen branching off in the distance.

GREENWOOD AVENUE, *c.* 1940. This postcard shows a busy day in downtown Bethel just prior to the start of World War II. The photograph was taken from a point close to where the Bethel Shoe Store stands today.

P.T. BARNUM SQUARE, 1941. The Booklet bookstore had just opened for business when this photograph was taken. The small, white building built in 1827 would continue to house this popular stop for bibliophiles for over fifty years.

PLUMTREES ROAD, 1906. This postcard depicts Plumtrees Road near the present intersection with Walnut Hill Road. Looking east, one can see the tracks of the old Shepaug Railroad line crossing the road.

THE SHEPAUG RAILROAD BRIDGE, 1906. Constructed in 1872, this bridge near the lower entrance to Whittlesey Drive allowed trains to cross Beaver Brook on their way to Hawleyville station in Newtown. From there, trains would connect with the Shepaug line that ran north to Litchfield. The Shepaug line was described as "slow, late and noisy," and was discontinued in 1911.

CORNER OF CHESTNUT STREET AND GREENWOOD AVENUE, 1910. When an army unit came to town for training exercises, the soldiers took time to water their horses at an old iron cistern. The large building behind the horses was once a hat factory and now serves as an apartment house.

THE DOUGHBOY STATUE, 1928. The grass island located in the heart of Bethel had remained empty for nearly five years prior to the date of this postcard while citizens debated what should replace the Barnum fountain. The statue was officially unveiled on Memorial Day, May 31, 1928.

PANORAMIC VIEW OF BETHEL, *c.* 1895. This remarkable wide-angle view of Bethel was taken from atop Eagle's Cliff and is comprised of three separate photographs that were later connected. It is difficult to pinpoint the exact year of this photograph, but there are some clues as to its date of origin. The Center School—constructed in 1894—is shown toward the middle, so the photograph could not have been taken prior to 1894. As the landscaping around the old

GREENWOOD AVENUE, *c.* 1900. At the time of this photograph the horse and buggy had yet to be supplanted by the horseless carriage. This scene shows the area just in front of what is now P.T. Barnum Square. The building that was at this time occupied by Lynch's Market, among other concerns, is now home to the Bethel Cycle Shop.

Center School shows more evidence of dirt than grass, it may indicate that this photograph was taken sometime shortly after the school's completion. On closer examination, one can perceive the Judd-Dunning Hat factory that stood where the Shannon Brothers service station is today. This hat factory burned in February 1909, so the photograph must have been taken before that time.

SIDEWALK STROLL, c. 1900. These women seem surprised to realize that they are being preserved for posterity. The photographer was probably stationed in a second-floor window of the Fox Brothers' Hotel, located diagonally across the street.

CHINAMAN'S HILL, *c.* 1940. This portion of Greenwood Avenue between Rector Street and the current entrance to the Bethel Food Market was at one time known as Chinaman's Hill because of a Chinese laundry which was located here for many years. The building at left is now the Bethel Music Center and was part of the original wood-frame Center School.

GREENWOOD AVENUE, *c.* 1939. This photograph shows the area across from the Bethel Methodist Church during the Christmas shopping season. Containers of fruits and vegetables from the First National supermarket, then located at 120 Greenwood Avenue, can be seen on the sidewalk.

Two
People in Motion

CIVIL WAR SOLDIERS, 1864. Officers of the 23rd Regiment, Connecticut Volunteers, appear here in New Orleans in 1864 after their release from a thirteen-month imprisonment in Tyler, Texas. The Bethel men were: George S. Crofut (first row, second from left); Charles K. Bailey (second row, second from left); and Oscar H. Hibbard (second row, second from right).

BETHEL GUN CLUB, *c.* 1900. This group of Bethel marksmen once practiced their skills at a site along Judd Avenue, close to where the entrance to the Educational Park now exists.

BETHEL HOME GUARD, 1918. The Bethel Home Guard was a military group formed during World War I in order to provide protection, if needed, on the homefront. The site is Parloa Field and a sizable number of patriotic citizens are obviously in attendance.

BETHEL HOME GUARD, 1918. Here we see the home guard posed on the front steps of what was then the Congregational Church House, a building now known as the Masonic Temple.

BETHEL WOMEN IN DRAMATIC PRODUCTION, c. 1910. This gathering of female Bethelites took place in what was then the Seelye homestead and is now the Bethel Public Library. The play involved two young women conversing with some of the great heroines of history.

BETHEL BASEBALL CLUB, 1903. Bethel boasted its own team of sandlot sluggers when this photograph was taken on June 13, 1903. The center figure in the back row has been identified as John McCorkell, the team's manager.

BETHEL BASEBALL CLUB, 1903. This photograph provides another interesting view of local baseball at the turn of the century. Uniforms and equipment have changed somewhat over time. Games were held at the old Henry Street grounds; a game against Danbury held on September 19, 1904, attracted a crowd of 3,100 spectators.

BASKETBALL TEAM, 1929. The Bethel High School girls' basketball team for the 1928–29 school year poses proudly in their stylish uniforms.

BETHEL HIGH SCHOOL FOOTBALL TEAM, c. 1904. Helmets were optional, it appears, when this photograph of young Bethel gridiron heroes was taken. The player making the snap is Morris Britto, who went on to serve as Bethel's chief of police for many years.

THE BETHEL DRUM CORPS, 1883. The Bethel Drum Corps was a regular at all events of importance in Bethel from the year of this photograph up until the late 1950s. Here the corps is shown posing proudly in their first set of uniforms.

BETHEL DRUM CORPS, 1896. The corps had acquired new uniforms by the time this photograph was taken, thirteen years after the group's formation.

BETHEL DRUM CORPS, *c.* 1920. The corps is shown here marching along West Street in Danbury. In the background can be seen the Taylor Opera House, which was destroyed by fire in 1922.

BETHEL CORNET BAND, *c.* 1880. The twenty-three-member marching band, which preceded the Bethel Drum Corps, poses on West Street in Danbury after a parade performance. They must have made an impressive sound.

BETHEL CORNET BAND, 1880. These musicians were on hand to perform at Bethel's celebration of the national centennial in 1876. This photograph was taken in Danbury just before the band left for Brewster, New York, to fill one of its first out-of-town engagements.

ELM STREET (NOW GREENWOOD AVENUE), 1894. In order to accommodate the track being laid for the new electric trolley, the great elm tree that had given Elm Street its name was removed. On the night of the tree's removal, a man driving a horse and wagon drove his conveyance into the hole caused by the excavation and was killed.

FAY-GORMAN HAT FACTORY FIRE, 1913. On August 26, 1913, one of Bethel's oldest and largest hat factories caught fire and was extensively damaged. Workmen tarring the roof accidentally ignited the quick-spreading fire, but luckily the building was vacant at the time of the conflagration.

RUINS OF THE CLARK BOX SHOP FOLLOWING FIRE, 1913. A factory that produced boxes in which many of Bethel's hats were shipped was burned by a serial arsonist who came to be known as "the firebug." The building stood close to the existing entrance of the Bethel Food Market.

TREE TRANSPLANT, *c.* 1890. This scene shows a team of horses transporting a large tree near the corner of Greenwood Avenue and Oxford Street. The figure in the center wearing a derby is thought to be Edgar T. Andrews.

PUTNAM PARK, *c.* 1906. Students and faculty happily posed for a group photograph while enjoying a Sunday school picnic sponsored by the Bethel Methodist Church.

METHODIST SUNDAY SCHOOL CLASS, *c.* 1870. A group of fashionably attired young ladies from the Bethel Methodist Church are shown posing for their portrait at Couch's Photograph Studio in Danbury.

BETHEL CENTER CEMETERY, 1925. Memorial Day exercises were held at the town's Civil War Monument on May 30, 1925, with the few remaining veterans of the war between the states in attendance.

BETHEL CENTER CEMETERY, *c.* 1900. The Danbury Wooster Lodge and the Bethel Putnam Lodge of the Knights of Pythias were in attendance for this formal portrait taken near the Civil War Monument. The gentleman shown in the center, wearing a sword, is Civil War veteran Charles K. Bailey, who was instrumental in instituting memorial services in town.

DOUGHBOY STATUE, 1928. May 31, 1928, was a big day in Bethel as a statue properly entitled "The Spirit of the American Doughboy" was first unveiled. Created by artist E.M. Viquesney, the statue is said to have inspired eighty look-alikes throughout the nation, including one in Canaan, Connecticut.

GOVERNOR'S VISIT, *c.* 1899. This photograph presents a unique view of a visit by Governor George E. Lounsbury of Ridgefield, in office from 1899 to 1901. His carriage is stopped along Greenwood Avenue near what is today the Bethel Cycle Shop. The gentleman standing to the right of the carriage, with hat in hand, is the Reverend Henry L. Slack of the Congregational church.

PLANE CRASH, 1934. At 12:55 am on Memorial Day, 1934, a United Airlines aircraft crashed in a wooded area just off Taylor Avenue. As a result of quick thinking by area residents, the nine passengers and three crew members were transported to Danbury Hospital and all survived.

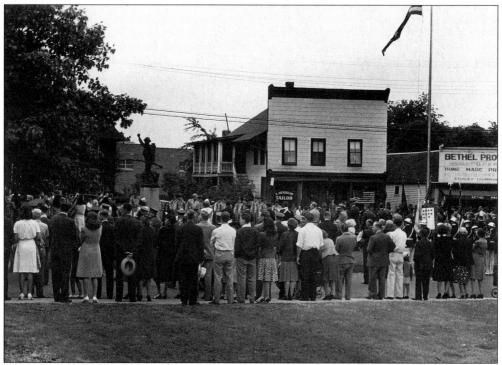

MEMORIAL DAY SERVICES, c. 1943. World War II made Bethelites more conscious of the importance of patriotism, as evidenced by the large turnout for ceremonies held at P.T. Barnum Square.

Three
Pride of Place

JOHN KEANE HOUSE, *c.* 1930. This old saltbox house was probably one of Bethel's earliest dwelling places. Until the mid-1960s it stood at 9 Grassy Plain Street just past the entrance to the former Dolan Gravel Bank. It was in this house that the first Roman Catholic mass was celebrated in Bethel, sometime around 1845.

NATHANIEL BENEDICT HOUSE, c. 1948. This home, located on Hawleyville Road in the Stony Hill district, is believed to have been built by Nathaniel Benedict in about the year 1765. For many years the home was known as the "Major Dikeman Place" for an owner whose family retained possession from 1820 to 1908.

THOMAS TAYLOR HOUSE, c. 1948. This home on Milwaukee Avenue was originally owned by Thomas Taylor and was most likely built in the 1770s. It later became the property of his son, Captain Eli Taylor, a Revolutionary War veteran. Captain Taylor's daughter married Colonel John Lyman Andrews and the property was retained by the Andrews family for many years.

JABEZ TAYLOR HOUSE, 1934. This home, dating to about 1782 and located atop Hoyt's Hill, was in later years known as the Old Larson Farm. It was situated on a large tract of land that afforded a commanding view of downtown Bethel and the surrounding countryside.

DANIEL HICKOK HOUSE, c. 1896. This home, which still stands on Blackman Avenue, is reputed to have been host to Generals Benedict Arnold, David Wooster, and Gold Selleck Silliman on the night of April 26, 1777, as the British were burning Danbury.

DANIEL HICKOK JR. HOUSE, *c.* 1896. This stately home once stood on the corner of Maple and Hickok Avenues. The home was torn down in the 1950s to make way for a Connecticut Light and Power substation.

ELIAKIM STARR HOUSE, *c.* 1896. This saltbox house at 27 Grassy Plain Street still survives today despite many changes and a recent fire. Once referred to as "the Old Eliakim Starr Place," the house may have been built by Eliakim's father, Captain Josiah Starr, as early as 1739.

STEPHEN TROWBRIDGE HOUSE, *c*. 1910. This house at 63 Grassy Plain Street is said to have been built in 1734 and as such is one of the earliest surviving homes in Bethel. At the time of this photograph the house was owned by John P. Gorman. Two members of the Gorman family are shown in front.

STAIB HOUSE, *c*. 1896. This saltbox home once stood just east of King Lake in the Elmwood district. In March of 1910, when the property was owned by F.M. Barrell, the house and its contents were destroyed by fire.

JERUSHA WHEELER HOMESTEAD, *c.* 1890. This ancient dwelling stood at 39 Grassy Plain Street and was for many years home to a woman named Jerusha Wheeler. P.T. Barnum once boarded here and it was in this house that he met his first wife, Charity Hallet, on a rainy night in 1826.

BENJAMIN HICKOK HOMESTEAD, 1899. This home, believed to have been built by Ebenezer Hickok in about the year 1760, is said to have served as a tavern run by Benjamin Hickok during the American Revolution. At the time this photograph was taken on February 15, 1899, the home was owned by George B. Fairchild.

P.T. BARNUM'S BIRTHPLACE, *c.* 1910. It was here at 55 Greenwood Avenue that P.T. Barnum was born to Philo and Irena Barnum on July 5, 1810. A fire sometime in the 1840s destroyed the front portion of the home, leaving only the kitchen and woodhouse. The house was renovated and Barnum's mother continued to reside here until her death in 1868.

SEELYE HOMESTEAD, 1910. When this postcard was produced, the Seelye home was not yet in use as a public library. In July of 1914, the Greek Revival home, built in 1842, became town property as provided for in the will of Hannah H. Seelye. The library, which has been greatly expanded, continues to serve the public to this day.

BETHEL PUBLIC LIBRARY, *c.* 1920. A large sign proudly proclaimed that Bethel had achieved the long-sought dream of having its own free public library. A cornfield at left and two barns to the rear suggest that Bethel was still very much a small town.

JABEZ TROWBRIDGE HOUSE, *c.* 1890. This home, built around 1800, stood on Grassy Plain Street near the present entrance to Cherry Lane. The structure was torn down in 1891 to make way for a larger Victorian-style home that still exists.

SQUIRE THOMAS TAYLOR HOME, 1890. This stately Italianate-style home, at what is now 158 Greenwood Avenue, was owned by one of Bethel's wealthiest citizens, Thomas Taylor. In 1920 the house was purchased for use by the Knights of Columbus, and was dramatically altered. Today the building is home to Parker East Dry Goods, Brew Master's Pub Sport Ltd., and Dr. Mike's Ice Cream Shop.

KNIGHTS OF COLUMBUS HALL, c. 1930. Unbelievably, this building is the same one shown in the previous photograph. The home's original hipped roof, topped by a large cupola, was replaced by a gabled one, and an addition was created on the building's right side. The front veranda was then redesigned and shake shingles were added to the exterior.

OLD JUDD HOMESTEAD, *c.* 1885. The house shown in this photograph still stands on Maple Avenue, although the large farm that once surrounded it has been filled in by a sizable number of newer homes.

SQUIRES HOMESTEAD, *c.* 1895. This pretty Victorian cottage remains to this day at the corner of Grassy Plain and South Streets. Mrs. Squires, shown on the front lawn, would lose her husband and both of her daughters to disease in 1913, while she would live on to the age of ninety, dying in 1955.

GEORGE A. HICKOK HOME,
c. 1885. This large Victorian house
was home to one of Bethel's leading
hat manufacturers. Today this spot, at
the northwest corner of Greenwood
Avenue and Chestnut Street, is home
to a service station and convenience
store.

NO. 48 GREENWOOD AVENUE,
c. 1900. This beautiful home in
downtown Bethel still exists today
with some alterations. The group
gathered on the front veranda is
believed to consist of members of the
Patchen family.

CHARLES K. BAILEY HOME, 1876. This house at 45 Greenwood Avenue was once owned by Luther Holcomb, who, according to legend, single-handedly stopped a British invasion force atop Hoyt's Hill during the Revolution. Later it was home to Charles K. Bailey, a Civil War veteran. The Bailey and Keeler families, along with Timothy B. Hickok, are shown here.

NEHEMIAH B. CORNING HOMESTEAD, c. 1870. Nehemiah B. Corning was a prosperous dealer in coal and wood who lived in this stately home at what is currently 120 Greenwood Avenue. The house was torn down to make way for a large commercial building that today houses the Bethel Cycle Shop.

OLD DIBBLE HOMESTEAD, *c.* 1880. This home on Walnut Hill Road in the Stony Hill district was built in about 1850 by Samuel Dibble on the site of a 1740 house that had been moved. The figure at right may be William E. Dibble. The original negative of this photograph was apparently reversed.

ISRAEL H. WILSON HOTEL, *c.* 1890. This large home at 4 Chestnut Street was built in the late 1700s and was once a tavern operated by P.T. Barnum's grandfather, Phineas Taylor, and later by his parents, Philo and Irena Barnum. Afterward it became a temperance house; still later it was known as the Wilson Hotel. Israel H. Wilson is the figure on the far left.

ORRIN BENEDICT HOME, *c.* 1890. This carefully staged photograph shows the magnificent home of one of Bethel's wealthiest and most influential hat manufacturers, Orrin Benedict. The elaborate Italianate-style mansion stood close to where the Sycamore Restaurant is today.

WILLIAM H. BARNUM HOME, *c.* 1890. This home was first built by hat manufacturer Orrin Benedict. It was later sold to Benedict's business partner, William H. Barnum. The home stood on the ground that now encompasses the parking lot of the Brooks Pharmacy on Greenwood Avenue.

THE GEORGE G. DURANT HOME, *c.* 1910. This elegant lawn party was held at 19 South Street, the home of wealthy hat manufacturer George G. Durant. The dwelling once had what was probably the longest veranda of any house in town.

BETHEL COMMUNITY HOUSE, 1921. This large brick building was completed in 1912 as the Congregational Church House. At the time of this postcard, the building was in use as a silent movie theater and a sign at the right of the front steps advertises the current attraction. The building became the Masonic Temple in 1927.

TERRY LUMBER YARD, 1932. This once-thriving enterprise stood at the end of Elizabeth Street, across from the old railroad station. The business closed down in 1972.

FIRST NATIONAL SUPERMARKET, 1942. The opening of this store at 137 Greenwood Avenue marked the arrival of Bethel's first self-service supermarket. Previous to this, shoppers relied upon the grocer to service their shopping needs from behind a counter.

GREENWOOD AVENUE
RAILROAD CROSSING,
c. 1942. Crossing gates were hand-
cranked at this point in time. A
proposal to introduce electric gates
during the time of the Great
Depression had been abandoned,
as it would have cost two men
their livelihoods.

BETHEL HIGH SCHOOL,
c. 1942. Built by the Public Works
Administration in 1939 as a way of
providing both a better educational
facility and needed construction
work, this building continues its
service to the town as a municipal
center.

BETHEL GENERAL STORE, *c.* 1900. This small store once stood at what is now 69 Greenwood Avenue. The two men in front of the store have been identified as Harry Plumb (on the left) and Charles K. Trowbridge (on the right).

BETHEL PHARMACY, *c.* 1890. Charles J. English (on the right) began a long family tradition when he opened his pharmacy in a building, erected in 1887, that came to be known as the English Brothers' Block. The building's address is now 134 Greenwood Avenue; it is currently occupied by the Totally Random store.

ENGLISH'S DRUG STORE, *c.* 1910. The former Bethel Pharmacy first debuted as English's Drug Store on December 20, 1905. Souvenir boxes of candy and bottles of perfume were presented to the ladies who called during the store's grand opening. The brothers E. Ambrose and Charles J. English Jr. are shown here.

ENGLISH'S DRUG STORE, *c.* 1910. This photograph provides a rare interior view of a pharmacy from days gone by. The gentleman behind the counter at left is Charles J. English Jr.

FRENCH'S GROCERY STORE, *c.* 1910. Situated at what is now 120 Greenwood Avenue, French's Grocery and Dry Goods Store and Dean's Market were the places where much of Bethel did its shopping. Frank B. French can be seen standing in the doorway of his store while Harry Dean is to the extreme right in his butcher's apron.

SQUIRES STATIONARY STORE, 1912. Located at what would now be 150 Greenwood Avenue, this stationery store run by Mr. and Mrs. Charles Squires sold all of the latest newspapers and magazines as well as postcards featuring local views. A sign in the window advertises an event to be held at Nichol's Opera House on Monday evening, September 30, 1912.

LUNCH ROOM, c. 1900. Coffee cost only 5¢ when John Hines operated this lunch room at the corner of Greenwood Avenue and Front Street. The bottom of the menu sign includes the words "Wait for the Car," suggesting that patrons have a bite to eat while in anticipation of the next available trolley.

BILLIARD PARLOUR, c. 1895. This rather scruffy group of characters is positioned outside what is now 180 Greenwood Avenue, a spot currently occupied by the Alpine Delicatessen. To the extreme left can be seen a sign identifying the Fox Brothers' Hotel.

BILLIARD PARLOUR, c. 1890. This scene may depict the billiard parlour once housed at 180 Greenwood Avenue, although there was another such establishment run by John F. Nichols on the first floor of the opera house at about the same time.

MORRISON AND DUNHAM HAY, FEED & GRAIN, c. 1915. This site at 201 Greenwood Avenue was once an important stop for Bethel's many farmers. It is now home to the Tremson Auto Parts store.

WALKER FERRY'S SHOE STORE, *c.* 1890. This still-extant three-story building at 12 Chestnut Street, dating from before 1851, was once owned by Walker Ferry. It housed his shoe store, McDowell's Meat Market, and a two-level residence.

BUTCHER'S SHOP, *c.* 1920. The exact location of this photograph is unknown, as there were four different butcher shops in town during this era. The shop shown may have been the popular establishment run by Theodore Brauneis at what is now 230 Greenwood Avenue.

DAVEY BROTHERS STORE, 1929. This small market was located on 1 Elm Street (now 75 Greenwood Avenue) and was managed by Daniel W. Light, shown at left. These were the days when customers could warm themselves by a pot-bellied stove while discussing local news.

Four

The Hatters

OLD HAT SHOP, c. 1948. This dilapidated structure was once the hat shop of Daniel Parsons Shepard and Son, which stood on the south side of Starr Road close to Route 58. Shepard, who lived from 1790 to 1863, presumably began business here sometime around 1820. The shop's sign went undisturbed for well over a century.

BETHEL HAT MANUFACTORY, *c.* 1867. This large structure, nicknamed the "Shanghai" hat factory, as well as the adjoining factory of David Comstock, once stood alongside the railroad tracks where the Bethel Central Texaco station and the Tremson Auto Parts store are today. Both buildings were destroyed by fire in August of 1867.

ORRIN BENEDICT'S SECOND HAT FACTORY, 1867. After his first factory burned in 1866, Benedict built this large wooden building, only to have it burn in 1872. His next building was built of brick as a precautionary measure. This building stood in the area now occupied by the Bethel Cinema.

EDWIN SHORT HAT FACTORY, *c.* 1896. In 1890 Edwin Short purchased Orrin Benedict's third hat factory. This firm was the largest in all of Bethel, employing between 150 to 175 workers, most of whom are shown here outside their place of work.

A. PHILLIPS & COMPANY FACTORY, *c.* 1920. From 1920 to 1923 the old Edwin Short hat factory served as the home of a business that city directories identified as "manufacturers of overgaiters, leggins and house slippers."

MOHAWK HAT FACTORY, *c.* 1961. The last known occupant of the building Orrin Benedict had built back in 1872 was the Mohawk Hat Company Incorporated, which was listed at this address from 1942 to 1960. The abandoned structure was destroyed by fire on May 16, 1965.

"THE GOLD MINE" HAT SHOP, *c.* 1876. Built by Frederick Mackenzie Sr. and Benjamin Crofut in about the year 1868, this hat shop on Nashville Road made its original owners so much money it became known as the "the Gold Mine" shop.

"THE GOLD MINE" HAT SHOP, c. 1881. Thomas C. Millard became associated with the factory in about the year 1881 and, as can be seen when this photograph is compared with the previous one, the business was enlarged.

"THE GOLD MINE" HAT SHOP, c. 1884. The factory was once again enlarged around this time, but the firm moved shortly thereafter to Danbury, leaving its Bethel workers behind.

JUDD & DUNNING SHOP CREW, *c.* 1890. This group photograph was taken in front of a hat factory that once stood at 82 Greenwood Avenue. The owners are shown standing in the third row on the left, and were (from left to right) Julius B. Judd, Howard Judd, and Henry Clay Judd.

JUDD & DUNNING SHOP CREW, *c.* 1885. Here we see the shop's workers lined up along the side of their factory as well as peering from its windows.

RUINS OF THE JUDD-DUNNING HAT FACTORY, 1909. On the night of March 22, 1909, a fire that apparently started in the boiler room at the rear of the factory put an end to this business. Some of the workers who were left unemployed by the disaster had served the company for nearly forty years.

BETHEL HAT FORMING COMPANY, *c.* 1885. This photograph shows workers outside a hatting business that stood at 93 Greenwood Avenue from its construction in 1860 until it burned in October of 1897. The factory was in operation at the time of the fire but all of its employees escaped unharmed.

EDWIN SHORT HAT FACTORY WORKERS, *c.* 1910. This photograph must have been taken on a day off, as the workers were never this nattily attired during usual business hours.

EDWIN SHORT SHOP CREW, *c.* 1895. A somber group of workmen take a break from their arduous labors only long enough to be snapped by a traveling photographer. Framed copies of the resulting photograph were then sold to interested workers for 30¢ apiece.

ANDREWS-MACKENZIE HAT COMPANY SHOP CREW, *c.* 1890. Hatting was dirty and difficult work, but many of these rugged workers still managed a smile for the camera.

BAIRD HAT FACTORY, *c.* 1910. This large hatting establishment on Main Street was run by John H. Baird at the time this postcard was created. It would also be known as the Melton Hat Company and later the Barton Rough Hat Company before its demolition in April of 1969. Its former location is now the site of the Phineas Apartments.

THE GEORGE HICKOK HAT FACTORY, *c.* 1885. This factory stood on Nashville Road in front of the old Center School. It operated from 1868 until June of 1894. In 1895 the building and grounds were sold to the town, which demolished the factory and added the land to the Center School grounds.

TYLER & LYON HAT FACTORY, *c.* 1885. This long gambrel-roofed establishment stood on Chestnut Street just across from the old Center School.

JOHN H. HAITSCH & COMPANY HAT FACTORY, *c.* 1930. This factory stood at the point where Nashville Road and Chestnut Street divide. The location was later used as a cider mill.

JUDD & ANDREWS HAT FACTORY SHOP CREW, *c.* 1890. The crew sits in front of a large factory that once stood near the point where Milwaukee Avenue connects with Maple Avenue. The factory seems to have been destroyed sometime around 1914.

JUDD & ANDREWS HAT TRIMMERS, *c.* 1910. Women played an essential role in the hatting process. They were assigned the job of "trimming" the hat by stitching in the liner, sweat band, and ribbons, which gave the hat its finished appearance.

COLE & AMBLER SHOP CREW, *c.* 1885. These hatters are lined up in front of a hat shop that had its origins in the late 1700s. The factory stood at the present-day location of P.T. Barnum Square and would continue in use until a devastating fire in 1913.

COLE & AMBLER FACTORY, c. 1880. George M. Cole and Samuel S. Ambler first went into business together at this location in 1868. Their successful partnership would continue until Cole's retirement in 1896. As evidenced by this photograph, their factory was one of the town's largest employers.

EDWIN SHORT HAT FACTORY, 1910. It required a large number of trimmers to meet the demands of a large hatting concern like the one operated by Edwin Short. The three figures in front are identified as the forelady and two foremen.

EDWIN SHORT FACTORY, *c.* 1896. Bicycling was very popular with "modern" women when this group of hat trimmers gathered for their portrait. The small boy at right seems to have been a bit of a ham.

ANDREWS-MACKENZIE TRIMMERS, *c.* 1893. These lady hatters did not believe in all work and no play. The trimmers are shown gathered together in a grove near their plant during a lunch hour respite from their tedious work.

GEORGE A. SHEPARD HAT LEATHER FACTORY, *c.* 1910. This photograph provides a rare view inside a factory that produced the leather sweatbands of hats. Unlike those of most factories associated with hatting, the employees shown here are predominately female. The owner, George A. Shepard, can be seen in the center wearing a derby.

GEORGE A. SHEPARD FACTORY, *c.* 1890. At the time of this photograph, the George A. Shepard and Son Company was still producing hatter's furs as well as trimmings. Shepard first began his business in 1867. As the hatting industry declined, Shepard's Incorporated, a moving and storage company, replaced the original business at its home on Henry Street.

FRANK CLARK BOX FACTORY, *c.* 1900. This factory produced paper boxes for the shipment of soft hats. The plant stood upon ground now occupied by the entrance to the Bethel Food Market. The building was burned by "the firebug" in 1913.

Five
Reading, Writing, and 'Rithmetic

WOLFPITS SCHOOLHOUSE, c. 1910. This small, one-room school once stood on Sunset Hill Road just north of the entrance to Aunt Patty's Lane. The teacher is identified simply as "Mrs. Judd."

STONY HILL SCHOOLHOUSE, c. 1920. This is the only known photograph of the school that once stood at the point where Vail and Hawleyville Roads meet. The school was closed in 1940 and was demolished about 1955. An ancient sycamore tree on a small island of grass now exists close to the school's former site.

CENTER SCHOOL, c. 1898. The Buster Brown style of dress was in vogue when this photograph was taken of Miss Lizzie Hayes and her pupils seated on the front steps of their school. The building had been opened in 1895 and had a twin structure on Grassy Plain Street.

GRASSY PLAIN SCHOOL, c. 1900. Having your school photograph taken meant dressing up when this group gathered at the turn of the century.

CENTER SCHOOL, c. 1900. Discipline problems were not tolerated when you were being recorded for posterity. However, Miss Lizzie Hayes seems to have things firmly under control.

CENTER SCHOOL, c. 1890. This large class met at the wood-frame structure that comprised the Center School before a larger brick building was opened in 1895. The teacher is thought to be Miss Ina Mansfield.

GRASSY PLAIN SCHOOL, c. 1890. This wood-frame school stood on the south side of Griswold Street, near the corner of Greenwood Avenue, before the opening of the newer school on Grassy Plain Street in 1895.

SCHOOL DAYS, *c.* 1920. Miss Lizzie Hayes seems to have gathered some gray hairs courtesy of the many pupils she educated over the years. The schoolhouse has not been identified.

GRASSY PLAIN SCHOOL, *c.* 1890. Their names have been lost to history but this group certainly showed promise when having their class photograph taken toward the end of "the Gilded Age."

CENTER SCHOOL, 1913. It seems to have been a cold winter morning when this group of grade-schoolers was bundled up and taken outside to pose for a photograph.

BETHEL HIGH SCHOOL, 1914. The freshman class braved the elements to have their photograph taken on a brisk January morning. Their school was built on South Street in 1887 and continued to serve as a high school until 1939. Afterward, the building was converted for use as a firehouse.

BETHEL HIGH SCHOOL, 1914. The entire sophomore class filled the steps of the high school for this photograph taken in November 1914. It is apparent that the building had been painted since the previous school year.

BETHEL HIGH SCHOOL, 1915. Twenty-two young men and women comprised the senior class of Bethel High in 1915. The young men must have enjoyed school dances, as they were greatly outnumbered by the young women.

GRASSY PLAIN SCHOOL, c. 1896. This rare photograph shows the Grassy Plain School shortly after its completion. The large bell tower was used to call the students to attendance. Chickens can be seen roaming the lawn of the building at left.

High School, Bethel, Conn.

BETHEL HIGH SCHOOL, 1911. This postcard view shows the old school on South Street as it looked during its heyday. Two studious young women are seated on the steps at left.

PLUMTREES SCHOOL, 1923. Built in 1867 on land deeded to the town by Miss Eliza Benedict, this simple schoolhouse served Bethel students, including the author, until the year 1970. The original structure was enlarged in 1884 and modernized in 1957 to include indoor plumbing. A front entrance facing Taylor Road was also added at that time.

PLUMTREES SCHOOL, 1951. Traditionally painted white with gray shutters, this old school still stands today, although currently clad in a coat of red and white. To the right of the school can be seen the old well pump that was used before the introduction of indoor plumbing. An outhouse was located to the rear of the property.

Six

Sacred Places

CONGREGATIONAL CHURCH, *c.* 1905. This beautiful edifice was built in 1867 and still serves its parishioners today. To the left can be seen a building that served as the Congregational church from 1842 until 1865, when it was damaged by a windstorm. The building was then moved to the west side of the old burying ground and served as the town hall until 1939.

CONGREGATIONAL CHURCH, 1907. This postcard view shows the church after the tops of its two towers had been painted a darker color than the rest of the building. At this point in time the tracks of the Shepaug Railroad connecting link still ran perilously close to the front entrance.

METHODIST CHURCH, c. 1865. This very early photograph shows the Methodist church shortly after its completion in 1861. The tremendously tall spire may have fallen victim to a fire that struck the church in January of 1884. A second spire of a much lower height was utilized until 1943, when yet another design was implemented.

METHODIST CHURCH, *c.* 1910. The second spire design of the church can be seen here along with the parsonage, which was radically altered and enlarged in 1894.

Methodist Episcopal Church and Parsonage, Bethel, Conn.

METHODIST CHURCH, 1890. The interior of the church is shown here as it appeared when decorated for a Children's Day service. The structure is the oldest church in town still being used for regular services.

SAINT MARY'S ROMAN CATHOLIC CHURCH, *c.* 1900. Completed in 1883, this place of worship was in use until 1996. The church's stained-glass windows have been incorporated into the design of the new church built along Route 302.

SAINT THOMAS EPISCOPAL CHURCH, *c.* 1908. This church became Bethel's second house of worship when it was built in 1835. It stood until 1909 when it was demolished to make way for the newer church that is still currently in use.

SAINT THOMAS EPISCOPAL CHURCH, 1935. This second church was dedicated on January 16, 1910. The stone for its construction came from the outlying farms of the church's parishioners.

OLD BURYING GROUND, 1899. Bethel's oldest cemetery, located alongside the Congregational church, contains headstones dating back to the 1760s. The "Old Burying Ground" serves as the final resting place for over four hundred individuals, with the last burial taking place here in 1879.

CIVIL WAR MONUMENT, *c.* 1895. This impressive monument, situated near the entrance to the Center Cemetery on South Street, was first dedicated on May 30, 1892. The stone bears the names of thirteen Union soldiers and sailors from Bethel whose remains were never recovered. Three of the thirteen fell at the Battle of Gettysburg.

CENTER CEMETERY, *c.* 1900. For many years a fountain graced the grounds of the cemetery. The fountain has since disappeared and the area where it once stood has been utilized for burial space.

Seven

Getting Around

THE ENGINE "BETHEL," *c.* 1867. This photograph may have been taken to record the inaugural run of the "Bethel" along the Danbury & Norwalk line in 1867. The train has stopped in Danbury at the point where South Street and Great Pasture Road intersect. Notice the warning sign to the left that reads "Look out for the Locomotive."

BETHEL DEPOT, 1889. This is the only known photograph showing Bethel's original train station that was built in 1852 and destroyed by fire in 1898. The depot was of the same architectural style as the Danbury station, with the exception of it being one story rather than two. Engine #15 of the Housatonic line is shown here with its crew.

ENGINE #4, BETHEL DEPOT, c. 1890. Engineer Austin Wheeler is shown behind the controls of Engine #4 of the Shepaug, Litchfield & Northern line. The building now home to MacKenzie's Olde Ale House as well as a portion of the opera house can be seen in the background.

BETHEL DEPOT, c. 1915. The station seems deserted in this snapshot taken when the building was less than twenty years old. At far left can be seen the Bethel Rustic Work Company, which would later be known as Vaghi Woodworking.

BETHEL DEPOT, c. 1910. The roads were nothing but mud when this photograph was taken. The opera house can be seen in the distance.

SHEPAUG CONNECTING LINK, *c.* 1910. Main Street was a dangerous place to be when the train rumbled along its north side. The line would be discontinued in 1911, with the exception of occasional runs to the Judd-Andrews Hat Company on Milwaukee Avenue and the Plumtrees Lime Kiln on Plumtrees Road.

BETHEL DEPOT, 1953. The railroad lines were electrified at the time this calendar photograph was taken by Ruth H. Mallory. Electrification had first been introduced in 1925 and would end in 1961. The wires would be removed in 1965 but their poles still remain.

BETHEL DEPOT, *c.* 1955. The commuter parking lot gradually gained popularity as Bethel's population grew during the postwar years.

RAILROAD STATION

BETHEL DEPOT, *c.* 1955. A freight train stands at the station while a lone vehicle occupies the parking lot in this mid-1950s postcard view. This stop would see active service until early 1996, when a new station was built further north along the line.

HORSE TROLLEY AT THE END OF THE LINE, *c.* 1894. The Danbury and Bethel Horse Railway had its start in 1887 and transported Bethelites from this point at Fountain Place (now P.T. Barnum Square) to the center of Danbury and back.

DANBURY & BETHEL STREET RAILWAY CAR, *c.* 1895. On January 1, 1895, a new era began when the old horse trolley was replaced by an expanded electric line. Service was extended east from Fountain Place to the intersection of Milwaukee Avenue and East Street (now part of Greenwood Avenue). The building at left is the former office of the B.J. Dolan Company.

THE TROLLEY, *c.* 1900. It cost only 5¢ but also only went 8 miles per hour. All cars were equipped with advertising signs positioned near their roofline.

THE TROLLEY, *c.* 1900. The trolley is shown here stopped near the Greenwood Avenue railroad crossing. This photograph was obviously taken during the summer months as it presents an open-air car. The sign on the front of the car refers to Lake Kenosia, the trolley's furthest stop.

THE TROLLEY, *c. 1920*. The trolley is shown at the end of the line at Milwaukee Avenue and East Street. The motorman has been identified as John Ferris and the conductor as Horace Fallon. Not long after this photograph, the Danbury & Bethel Street Railway Company also came to the end of its line, going bankrupt in 1926.

FIRST AUTOMOBILE IN BETHEL, 1902. Mr. and Mrs. Horace L. Shepard Sr., along with their son, Horace Jr., must have caused quite a stir when they tooled through Bethel in this brand new 1902 Oldsmobile. The age of the automobile had arrived.

GEORGE G. DURANT, *c.* 1915. Age was not a factor for George G. Durant, who was in his seventies at the time of this photograph. Durant had become wealthy in both the hatting and real estate businesses. He was responsible for the cutting through of Fleetwood Avenue in 1887.

WILLIAM P. ENGLISH, *c.* 1910. "Gaddy" English, as he was called, operated a tobacco business that produced Seal of Connecticut and Silk Hat cigars. This early automobile was utilized to advertise his products. Notice the silk hat attached to the top of the car's radiator.

ICE WAGON, c. 1895. John M. Signor was a well-known figure about town in the days before refrigeration. His home and ice house were located at the corner of Main and Chestnut Streets and his ice pond was located along the Nashville Road Extension. Signor committed suicide in 1899.

BRIDGE REPAIR, c. 1905. Manual labor ruled the day when these workmen set about improving the bridge across Beaver Brook. Old maps show the brook being spanned by two bridges, one leading east along Plumtrees Road and the other heading northeast along Walnut Hill Road. The arch bridge of the Shepaug Railroad can be seen in the background.

Eight
Bethel's Firefighters

GRASSY PLAIN HOSE COMPANY, c. 1880. This group of stout firemen are shown gathered around their hand-drawn hose wheel. Hat manufacturer Orrin Benedict helped organize the company after his hat factory was destroyed by fire in 1866. He made sure that their firehouse was located directly across from his new plant on Greenwood Avenue.

EUREKA HOOK AND LADDER COMPANY #1, *c.* 1890. This group of firefighters, shown here standing near the town bandstand at the intersection of Main and Wooster Streets, was organized in 1886. Their first firehouse was located close to the Greenwood Avenue railroad crossing and their second, built in 1890, was on Elizabeth Street. Today the building is the American Legion Hall.

OLD FORGOTTEN ENGINE COMPANY, *c.* 1900. This group of costumed firemen from Bethel and Danbury was a crowd-pleaser at area parades at the turn of the century. This photograph was taken after one such event in New Milford. The small, hand-drawn pumper at right is now in the Bethel Fireman's Museum.

DANBURY FIREMAN'S PARADE, 1912. On September 12, 1912, Danbury held a parade for area fire companies. Marching along in this photograph is the Old Forgotten Company carrying a sign crediting Bethel as their hometown.

ALERT HOSE COMPANY #3, c. 1910. First organized in 1876, this fire company had its firehouse on Nashville Road in a building now owned by the Grassy Plain Drum Corps. The firemen stand once more by the "Old Forgotten" hand-drawn pumper.

ALERT HOSE COMPANY #3, *c.* 1900. The fire company is shown here assembled in front of their hose house on Nashville Road. The structure's tall hose tower can be seen in the background. The Grassy Plain hose house was said to have been the same size and style before it was destroyed by an arsonist on January 7, 1914.

BETHEL FIREHOUSE, *c.* 1942. The former high school on South Street was left vacant in 1939 upon completion of a newer facility. A sum of $5,400 was then appropriated to convert the old school into a suitable firehouse. In July of 1942 the conversion was complete, as shown in this photograph taken at about that time. The building was demolished in 1966.

Nine
Barnum's Fountain

BARNUM FOUNTAIN, *c.* 1899. P.T. Barnum purchased this fountain in Berlin, Germany, at a cost of around $7,500 and first placed it in the front of his Bridgeport mansion. It was soon found that the fountain caused a water-pressure problem in his home. After its presentation to Bethel, the fountain became a favorite place for photographs.

P.T. BARNUM, 1887. "The Great Showman," shown here with his great-grandson, Harry Rennel, was born in Bethel on July 5, 1810. He would return to his hometown many times during his colorful career and once stated that of all the places he had visited he "invariably cherished with the most affectionate remembrance the place of my birth."

BARNUM FOUNTAIN, 1881. This photograph was allegedly taken the day after Barnum officially presented the fountain to his native town. Rain on the day of the dedication made photography difficult, but despite the weather, a huge crowd turned out to hear Barnum deliver a speech that recalled his youth in Bethel.

BARNUM FOUNTAIN, *c.* 1890. Topped by an 18-foot figure of a triton blowing a conch shell, the fountain contained a small pool composed of three large shells balanced on the tailfins of dolphins who spewed water from their open mouths. A drinking fountain stood just in front of the basin. Fountain Place was then bordered by hat factories.

BARNUM FOUNTAIN, 1899. The fountain glistens in the sunlight on a warm summer's day. The drinking fountain seems to have become defunct by this point.

BARNUM FOUNTAIN, *c.* 1900. Less than twenty years after its debut, the fountain was already showing signs of neglect. Note that the drinking fountain is now gone and the guard rails and posts are somewhat bent. Litter can be seen along the curb.

BARNUM FOUNTAIN, *c.* 1905. Commercial buildings built between 1894 and 1895 can be seen to the right of the fountain. Also shown is the William C. Shepard home at far right. All of these structures survive to the present day.

BARNUM FOUNTAIN, *c.* 1908. This view of the fountain shows the downtown area looking west along Greenwood Avenue.

BARNUM FOUNTAIN, 1911. This photograph demonstrates how the electric trolley line (created in 1895) caused the street to encroach upon the front portion of the basin.

BARNUM FOUNTAIN, 1912. The fountain was shut off at the time of this photograph. A good deal of detail can be seen on the bodies of the dolphins.

BARNUM FOUNTAIN, c. 1920. Park benches and a new flagpole have been added, but the condition of the fountain itself appears to have worsened by the time of this postcard.

BARNUM FOUNTAIN, 1898. Pretty, yes, but also destructive. The many times that the fountain's waters were allowed to freeze over only hastened the landmark's own end. By the early 1920s it would cease to function and people began to view this relic of the Victorian age as an eyesore.

THE BARNUM FOUNTAIN'S SAD END, 1923. On October 17, 1923, the last remains of the fountain were smashed to pieces, and on the following day they were carted away. The bronze fragments were sold to a junk yard in Danbury, ironically located on Barnum Court. Here, the once-magnificent triton rests amongst a pile of old automobile tires and other rubbish.

FOUNTAIN CORNERSTONE, 1949. Police chief and historian Morris S. Britto exhibits the cornerstone of the fountain for an article that appeared in the *New York Herald Tribune* magazine on June 5, 1949. The current whereabouts of the cornerstone are unknown.